THE FAMILY
OF PARROTS

THE FAMILY
OF PARROTS

Illustrations by Edward Lear

AMERICAN MUSEUM OF NATURAL HISTORY • NEW YORK
POMEGRANATE ARTBOOKS • SAN FRANCISCO

Published by Pomegranate Artbooks
Box 6099, Rohnert Park, California 94927

Pomegranate Europe Ltd.
Fullbridge House, Fullbridge
Maldon, Essex CM9 7LE, England

ISBN 0-7649-0336-5
Pomegranate Catalog No. A883

Designed by Bonnie Smetts Design

Printed in Hong Kong
01 00 99 98 97 96   6 5 4 3 2 1

First Edition

Introduction

E dward Lear (1812–1888), the youngest of twenty-one children, was born into a prosperous family in Highgate, London. When he was thirteen, however, his father, Jeremiah Lear, declared bankruptcy and was sent to debtors' prison, and the family was broken apart. Edward went to live with his sister Anne, who was twenty-one years his senior. Although she was somewhat eccentric, she possessed a talent for drawing and taught her brother to draw and paint flowers, birds, and butterflies. Anne's lessons were the entire extent of Edward's art instruction, and his formal education in basic reading, writing, and arithmetic lasted only a few years. The siblings lived in poverty, eking out a living with their drawings. Fourteen-year-old Edward sold sketches in the streets, colored prints and fans, and drew "morbid diseases" for doctors and hospitals for a few pence. His frequent epileptic seizures added to the misery of their difficult lives.

Fortunately, Lear's drawings caught the attention of a number of influential naturalists, who were impressed with his work. His first bird drawing was published in 1830 in *The Gardens of the Zoological Society delineated.* At sixteen, Lear embarked on an ambitious and unique project—to draw all the known parrot species. The Zoological Society gave Lear permission to use the birds in the Gardens as models, and a keeper handled the parrots for him, encouraging the birds to preen, spread their wings, or sway. Day after day Lear sketched the parrots, observing each one's unique characteristics and carefully noting its plumage, coloration, and behavior. To his annoyance, visitors to the zoo stared at Lear with even more interest than at the parrots. The margins of his sketches are filled with humorous and sometimes malicious cartoons of his gaping audience. Over time, Lear's supply of models increased beyond the birds in the zoo: Lord Stanley, thirteenth earl of Derby and president of the Zoological Society, lent him parrots from his Knowsley menagerie, and fashionable ladies lent him their pet parrots.

Lear planned to publish his drawings in a fourteen-part folio. The result, *Illustrations of the family of Psittacidae, or parrots* (published in twelve parts, 1830–1832), was the first British publication on a single family of birds. He painstakingly transferred his designs onto heavy lithographic stones with greasy chalk and carried them to the shop of Charles Hullmandel, the finest printer in London. In the beginning, Lear was not aware that the images had to be drawn in reverse on the lithographic stone; as a result, his drawing of the scarlet macaw was printed facing in the wrong direction. As his own publisher, Lear oversaw the printing, hand-coloring, and distribution of the series—an incredible effort for an eighteen-year-old.

One hundred ten subscribers received installments of the *Parrots* through the spring of 1832, when Lear abandoned the project. Although his birds were well received, the young man could not financially support the completion of the work. Many subscribers did not pay in a timely manner; thus, Lear could not continue to meet production costs and keep food on the table. Although only forty-two parrot portraits were published, the excellence of Lear's paintings gained him work with John Gould, author of numerous large-format bird books, and a membership in the Linnaean Society.

In addition to contributing illustrations to Gould's monographs, Lear illustrated articles for *The Proceedings of the Zoological Society of London,* and Lord Stanley commissioned him to draw the animals and birds in his menagerie. These drawings were published in *Gleanings from the menagerie and aviary at Knowsley Hall* (1846). During his residence at Knowsley, Lear wrote nonsense verse to entertain Lord Stanley's grandchildren and illustrated the verses with caricatures, much to the children's delight.

By 1836, when Lear was just twenty-four, his eyesight

and general health had deteriorated to such an extent that he could no longer draw birds and animals to the exacting standards required for scientific illustration. The following year, he left England for Italy. He traveled in Egypt, Greece, Turkey, and India and throughout Europe, earning his living by painting landscapes and writing nonsense verse. He died peacefully in Italy in 1888. Today, Lear is best remembered as author of the children's poem "The Owl and the Pussycat."

Since only 175 copies of *Illustrations of the family of Psittacidae, or parrots* were published, the monograph is exceedingly rare today. The elegant portraits of the parrots capture each bird's individuality and personality. Depicted in accurate, vibrant color, with each type of feather carefully delineated, the birds are full of personality, shown preening, stretching, raising crests, or ruffling feathers. The glorious hand-colored illustrations are highlighted with egg white to give an eye "life" or to accentuate feathers. Some backgrounds are lightly sketched, while others just hint at foliage—all to highlight the parrots' extravagant beauty. The folio was issued without a letterpress (text).

Among the treasures of the Research Library of the American Museum of Natural History is a copy of Lear's *Parrots*. One hundred sixty years after its publication, the folio's fine paper is still pristine, and its colors are as vibrant as the day they were painted. Regrettably, the Library's copy is missing plate 11, the *Long-billed Parrakeet-Maccaw* [*sic*]; apparently, the plate was missing when the Library acquired the folio a century ago (although it has graciously been provided by the New York Public Library for this volume).

—*Nina J. Root*

THE FAMILY
OF PARROTS

PSITTACUS BADICEPS

Bay-headed Parrot

E. Lear del et lith.   Printed by C. Hullmandel

PLYCTOLOPHUS ROSACEUS.

Salmon-crested Cockatoo ⅔ Nat. Size.

PLYCTOLOPHUS GALERITUS.

Greater Sulphur-crested Cockatoo.

PLYCTOLOPHUS SULPHUREUS.

PLYCTOLOPHUS LEADBEATERI.

Leadbeater's Cockatoo.

CALYPTORHYNCHUS BAUDINII.

Baudin's Cockatoo.

MACROCERCUS ARACANGA.

Red and Yellow Macaw.

Life Size.

MACROCERCUS ARARAUNA.

Blue & Yellow Macaw.

MACROCERCUS HYACINTHINUS.

Hyacinthine Maccaw.

PSITTACARA PATAGONICA.

Patagonian Parrakeet Maccaw

PSITTACARA LEPTORHYNCHA.

Long-billed Parrakeet-Maccaw.

PSITTACARA NANA.

Dwarf Parrakeet Maccaw

NANODES UNDULATUS.

Undulated Parrakeet.

PLATYCERCUS ERYTHROPTERUS.

Crimson-winged Parrakeet.

Male. Adult.

PLATYCERCUS ERYTHROPTERUS.

Crimson winged Parrakeet

1 Female *2 Young Male*

PLATYCERCUS TABUENSIS.

Tabuan Parrakeet

PLATYCERCUS BAUERI.

Bauer's Parrakeet

PLATYCERCUS BARNARDI.

Barnard's Parrakeet

E. Lear del. et lith.   Printed by C. Hullmandel

PLATYCERCUS PALLICEPS.

Paleheaded Parrakeet.

In the possession of M. Landseer.

PLATYCERCUS BROWNII.

Brown's Parrakeet.

PLATYCERCUS PILEATUS.

Red-capped Parrakeet.

PLATYCERCUS PILEATUS.
Red-capped Parrakeet.
(female)
In the Possession of the Right Hon. Lord Stanley

PLATYCERCUS STANLEYII.

Stanley Parrakeet.

Young Male.

PLATYCERCUS STANLEYII.

Stanley Parrakeet.

PLATYCERCUS UNICOLOR.

Uniform Parrakeet.

PLATYCERCUS PACIFICUS.

Pacific Parrakeet.

PALÆORNIS NOVÆ-HOLLANDIÆ.

New Holland Parrakeet.

in the Collection of the Right Hon. the Countess of Mountcharles.

1. Male 2. Female.

PALÆORNIS MELANURA.

Black-tailed Parrakeet.

In the Collection of Mr. Leadbeater

PALÆORNIS ANTHOPEPLUS.

Blossom-feathered Parrakeet.

PALÆORNIS ROSACEUS.

Roseate Parrakeet.

PALÆORNIS COLUMBOIDES.

Pigeon Parrakeet

PALÆORNIS CUCULLATUS.

Hooded Parrakeet.

PALÆORNIS TORQUATUS.

Rose-Ringed Parrakeet, Yellow Variety.

TRICHOGLOSSUS ATRITORQUIS.

Scarlet collared Parrakeet

TRICHOGLOSSUS MACONI.

Macoi's Parrakeet.

TRICHOGLOSSUS VERSICOLOR.

Variegated Parrakeet.

LORIUS DOMICELLA.

Black-capped Lory.

PSITTACULA KUHLII.

Kuhl's Parrakeet

PSITTACULA TARANTA.

Abyssinian Parrakeet.

PSITTACULA TORQUATA.

Collared Parrakeet

PSITTACULA RUBRIFRONS.

Red Rumped Parrakeet.

PSITTACULA SWINDERNIANA.

Swindern's Parrakeet

Illustrations

The Family of Parrots

Compiled by Allison Andors, Ph.D., Department of Ornithology, American Museum of Natural History

Each entry below gives first the scientific and common names for the parrot as given on the plate, then the scientific and common names by which that bird is known today.

Page 15
Psittacus badiceps
Bay-headed Parrot
Now *Pionites leucogaster*
White-bellied Parrot

Page 16
Plyctolophus rosaceus
Salmon-crested Cockatoo
Now *Cacatua moluccensis*
Salmon-crested Cockatoo

Page 17
Plyctolophus galeritus
Greater Sulphur-crested Cockatoo
Now *Cacatua galerita*
Sulphur-crested Cockatoo

Page 18
Plyctolophus sulphureus
Lesser Sulphur-crested Cockatoo
Now *Cacatua sulphurea*
Yellow-crested Cockatoo

Page 19
Plyctolophus Leadbeateri
Leadbeater's Cockatoo
Now *Cacatua leadbeateri*
Pink Cockatoo

Page 20
Calyptorhynchus Baudinii
Baudin's Cockatoo
Now *Calyptorhynchus baudinii*
White-tailed Black-Cockatoo

Page 21
Macrocercus Aracanga
Red and Yellow Maccaw
Now *Ara macao*
Scarlet Macaw

Page 22
Macrocercus Ararauna
Blue and Yellow Maccaw
(Blue & Yellow Maccaw)
Now *Ara ararauna*
Blue-and-yellow Macaw

Page 23
Macrocercus hyacinthinus
Hyacinthine Maccaw
Now *Anodorhynchus leari*
Indigo Macaw

Page 24
Psittacara Patachonica (Psittacara Patagonica)
Patagonia Parrakeet Maccaw
Now *Cyanoliseus patagonus*
Burrowing Parakeet

Page 25
Psittacara leptorhyncha
Long-billed Parrakeet Maccaw
Now *Enicognathus leptorhynchus*
Slender-billed Parakeet

Rare Books and Manuscripts Division
The New York Public Library
Astor, Lenox, and Tilden Foundations

Page 26
Psittacara nana
Dwarf Parrakeet Maccaw
Now *Aratinga nana*
Olive-throated Parakeet

Page 27
Nanodes undulatus
Undulated Parrakeet
Now *Melopsittacus undulatus*
Budgerigar

Page 28
Platycercus erythropterus
Crimson-winged Parrakeet (adult male)
Now *Aprosmictus erythropterus*
Red-winged Parrot

Page 29
Platycercus erythropterus
Crimson-winged Parrakeet
(female and young male)
Now *Aprosmictus erythropterus*
Red-winged Parrot

Page 30
Platycercus Tabuensis
Tabuan Parrakeet
Now *Prosopeia tabuensis*
Red Shining-Parrot

Page 31
Platycercus Baueri
Bauer's Parrakeet
Now *Platycercus zonarius*
Port Lincoln Ringneck

Page 32
Platycercus Barnardi
Barnard's Parrakeet
Now *Platycercus barnardi*
Mallee Ringneck

Page 33
Platycercus palliceps
Pale-headed Parrakeet
(Paleheaded Parrakeet)
Now *Platycercus adscitus*
Pale-headed Rosella

Page 34
Platycercus Brownii
Brown's Parrakeet
Now *Platycercus venustus*
Northern Rosella

Page 35
Platycercus pileatus
Red-capped Parrakeet (adult male)
Now *Purpureicephalus spurius*
Red-capped Parrot

Page 36
Platycercus pileatus
Red-capped Parrakeet (female)
Now *Purpureicephalus spurius*
Red-capped Parrot

Page 37
Platycercus Stanleyii
Stanley Parrakeet (young male)
Now *Platycercus icterotis*
Western Rosella

Page 38
Platycercus Stanleyii
Stanley Parrakeet (adult male)
Now *Platycercus icterotis*
Western Rosella

Page 39
Platycercus unicolor
Uniform Parrakeet
Now *Cyanoramphus unicolor*
Antipodes Parakeet

Page 40
Platycercus pacificus
Pacific Parrakeet
Now *Cyanoramphus novaezelandiae*
Red-fronted Parakeet

Page 41
Palaeornis Novae Hollandiae
(*Palaeornis Novae-Hollandiae*)
New Holland Parrakeet
(male and female)
Now *Nymphicus hollandicus*
Cockatiel

Page 42
Palaeornis melanura
Black-tailed Parrakeet
Now *Polytelis anthopeplus*
Regent Parrot

Page 43
Palaeornis anthopeplus
Blossom-feathered Parrakeet
Now *Polytelis anthopeplus*
Regent Parrot

Page 44
Palaeornis rosaceus
Roseate Parrakeet
Now *Polytelis swainsonii*
Superb Parrot

Page 45
Palaeornis Columboides
Pigeon Parrakeet
Now *Psittacula columboides*
Malabar Parakeet

Page 46
Palaeornis cucullatus
Hooded Parrakeet
Now *Psittacula eupatria*
Alexandrine Parakeet

Page 47
Palaeornis torquatus
Rose-ringed Parrakeet (yellow variety)
Now *Psittacula krameri*
Rose-ringed Parakeet

Page 48
Trichoglossus rubritorquis
Scarlet-collared Parrakeet
Now *Trichoglossus rubritorquis*
Red-collared Lorikeet

Page 49
Trichoglossus Matoni
Maton's Parrakeet
Now *Trichoglossus chlorolepidotus*
Scaly-breasted Lorikeet

Page 50
Trichoglossus versicolor
Variegated Parrakeet
Now *Psitteuteles versicolor*
Varied Lorikeet

Page 51
Lorius Domicella
Black-capped Lory
Now *Lorius domicella*
Purple-naped Lory

Page 52

Psittacula Kuhlii
Kuhl's Parrakeet
Now *Vini kuhlii*
Kuhl's Lorikeet

Page 53

Psittacula Tarantae (Psittacula Taranta)
Abyssinian Parrakeet
Now *Agapornis taranta*
Black-winged Lovebird

Page 54

Psittacula torquata
Collared Parrakeet
Now *Bolbopsittacus lunulatus*
Guaiabero

Page 55

Psittacula rubrifrons
Red-fronted Parrakeet
Now *Loriculus philippensis*
Colasisi

Page 56

Psittacula Swinderniana
Swindern's Parrakeet
Now *Agapornis swindernianus*
Black-collared Lovebird

References

Forshaw, Joseph M., illustrated by William T. Cooper. 1978. Parrots of the world. Second [revised] edition. Melbourne: Lansdowne Editions.

Lear, Edward. 1832. Illustrations of the family of Psittacidae, or parrots. . . . London: E. Lear.

Monroe, Burt L., and Charles G. Sibley. 1993. A world checklist of birds. New Haven and London: Yale University Press.

Peters, James Lee. 1937. Check-list of birds of the world. Volume III. Cambridge, USA: Harvard University Press.

Salvadori, T. 1891. Catalogue of the Psittaci, or parrots, in the collection of the British Museum. Catalogue of the birds in the British Museum, Volume XX. London: Trustees, British Museum (Natural History).

Sibley, Charles G., and Burt L. Monroe Jr. 1990. Distribution and taxonomy of birds of the world. New Haven and London: Yale University Press.